The Smell of the Light

© 2017 by Bill McCloud
All rights domestic and international retained by the author.
Published 2017 by The Balkan Press
First Edition
ISBN: 978-0-9979010-6-1
Author photo: Tim Bonea

Printed in the U.S.A.

No part of this book may be reproduced, scanned, or distributed in any printed or electronic form without permission. Please do not participate in or encourage piracy of copyrighted materials in violation of the author's rights. Purchase only authorized editions.

The Smell of the Light: Vietnam, 1968-1969

Bill McCloud

Author of What Should We Tell Our Children About Vietnam?

BALKAN PRESS

These poems are dedicated to those who came before:
my mom, F.D. Brown, and Grandma Winnie

Those who were there:
Vaughn Crayton and Tim Young

Those who have come along since:
William and Claudia, Cat and Maddy, and Samuel

"Everything's going to be OK."

Words Robert F. Kennedy spoke to Juan Romero, who cradled Kennedy's head after the senator and presidential candidate was shot. It was June 5, 1968, and Kennedy would die the next day. It was my 75th day in South Vietnam.

TABLE OF CONTENTS

THIS IS HOW IT STARTED!   3

Let's Drop Out   5

IN THE ARMY, BUT BEFORE VIETNAM   7

Six Things I Learned in Basic Training	9
Follow Instructions Exactly	10
No Ticket Out	11
Peace	12
Joe Salazar	13
Pay Check	14
Guard Duty	15
John Wayne	16
"C.O."	17
Assignment Day	18
Walter Cronkite Pulls Out	19
Off to War	20
Cleaned Out	21

VIETNAM   23

Plane Load of Pornography	25
Vung Tau I (The Luckiest Guy)	26
Vung Tau II (The Safest Place)	27
Arms Room	28
Chinooks	29
The Worst, Man!	30
Two (Army) Officers/Two (Bar) Girls	31
Beer Alchemy	33
Hooch Maids	34

I Shall Not Seek …	35
April Fool's	38
Leprosarium	39
The Disappearing Face	40
Tortoise	41
Eating Glass	42
Hillclimber 027	43
June 2, 1968	44
Bobby Kennedy	45
Darker Than Amber	46
Dylan Wins the War	47
Numbers	48
Fighting Fire	49
Oh, the Humanity!	50
Home Front	51
27 Hits	52
Sometimes You Just Can't Catch a Break	53
Betty and Veronica	54
How's Your VD Lately?	55
A Ball of Flames	56
Pruess	57
Called Home by Death	58
Eight Rounds	59
Not Without a Hitch	60
Seats	61
Shit	62
Lonesome Cities	63
"Crazy Ralph"	64
Young and Distant Love	66
The Tall Man	68
Mockingbird	69
Dream	70
Message from Milo	71
Officers' Club	72

Conversion Day (C-Day)	73
Gun Men	74
Sydney, Australia	75
Rubber Soul	77
Room 6	78
Write Your Mom (The Blue Period)	79
Thanksgiving Message	80
Rat Fink	81
His Sister	82
Short	83
Let's Fight	84
Bar (War?) Wound	86
Mid-Air Accident	87
Commander's Christmas Message	88
A Christmas Prayer	89
Ann-Margret	90
Apollo 8	91
Weather in Hell	92
Worker Bees and Flies	93
Trip to Town	94
Sarah Lawrence	95
Radio Adventure	96
Wounds	97
War (The Longest Day)	98
Tragedy on the Airfield (The Day We Lost Weldon Hodges of Midland, TX)	99
Rockets	100
Last Two Weeks (The Chant)	101
A Story I Never Enjoy Telling	102
Distinction	104
My Vietnam Experience	105

IN THE ARMY, BUT AFTER VIETNAM 107

The Saint Christopher Medal (A Love Story) 109
Back in the World 110
Beer 111
Sleep 112
Pot (The Disappointment) 113
Dark Side of the Moon 114
Tranquility Base 115
My Lai 116
McTeague 117
Slow Motion 119

OUT OF THE ARMY 121

Air Medal 123
Platoon (Everyone's Vietnam is Different) 124
Her Son 125
At the Wall 126

TODAY 127

Vung Tau III (Today) 129
Disability 130
Linh Is Bored 131

TWO ADDITIONAL POEMS 133

Blue 135
America 136

ACKNOWLEDGEMENTS 139

ABOUT THE AUTHOR 143

INTRODUCTION

These poems carry the reader, chronologically, through my Vietnam War experience, beginning in the spring of 1967. Most of them were written in 2015 and 2016.

They are not simply based on the memories of an old man desperately trying to recall events, incidents, and people from fifty years ago. In my case I was able to use fifty-two letters that I wrote home to my parents from Vietnam and that my family still has.

Those letters provide the stories, personalities, detail, and emotion that were the basis of most of these poems. If those letters had not been written and saved it would not have been possible for me to write these poems. My memory was also aided by reading the history pages that are part of our unit's current webpage.

After dropping out of college in my second semester I volunteered for the Army and entered the service on the 90-day delay program. I was in uniform from September of 1967 until September of 1970. I was in Vietnam from March of 1968 until March of 1969, serving as flight operations coordinator for the 147th Assault Support Helicopter Company (Hillclimbers) on the airfield at Vung Tau.

Vung Tau, about 45 miles southeast of Saigon (now Ho Chi Minh City), was one of the major in-country R&R centers for American and allied troops and was long rumored to serve the same purpose for the Viet Cong.

3 The Smell of the Light

THIS IS HOW IT STARTED!

LET'S DROP OUT

One day I was carpooling to
college with four other guys
when suddenly one of them

not necessarily the smartest one
said let's drop out
and join the army

and that's what we did
My problem with that school was that
they graded very strictly on attendance

Only a short time later did I discover that
the army was a lot more serious about
attendance than that school ever was

IN THE ARMY, BUT BEFORE VIETNAM

SIX THINGS I LEARNED IN BASIC TRAINING

1. The importance of malaria pills.
2. How to follow monkeys in a jungle to look for food.
3. To avoid sex when outside the U.S. because the black rot is everywhere.
4. The black rot is incurable.
5. How to defend myself in hand-to-hand combat.
6. Not to be concerned about taking a life. We're not really fighting people just gooks dinks and slants.

(Sent with love from Fort Polk Louisiana September 1967)

FOLLOW INSTRUCTIONS EXACTLY

When I fired for qualification
on the M14 and M16 rifles
I scored as expert on both

That pretty well amazed me
because I had never hunted or
shot a weapon before in my life

I thought I must be a
natural some hotshot but
they had an explanation

I had no bad habits to
unlearn and followed
their instructions exactly

That would be my style
through three years
in this man's army

Do exactly as you're told
and you'll succeed here
And I folded into myself

NO TICKET OUT

One of the guys in
our company in basic
about six weeks in
shot himself in the foot

He admitted he did it
to get out of the army
Drill Sergeant called us
all together to assure us

the guy was most
definitely not getting out
and had some time in the
stockade coming as well

A few guys made fun of him
called him names they thought
made it seem like he wasn't
much of a man

After lights out there was
a brief discussion about
whether having the guts
to shoot yourself

indicated any sense of courage
After two or three days
his name was never
mentioned again

PEACE

How sorry would someone
have to be to steal a big
peace-symbol necklace
at Fort Gordon Georgia

I couldn't wear
it all the time
so I often left it
in my locker

One day I came back
and it had been stolen
probably the coolest thing
I owned naturally

For the rest of 1967
I kept my eyes open for a
soldier at Fort Gordon Georgia
wearing a big peace symbol

I figured he'd be pretty easy to spot
but I never saw a soldier
advertising for peace
at Fort Gordon Georgia

13   The Smell of the Light

JOE SALAZAR

One of my best buddies
while stationed at Fort Gordon
over there in Georgia
was a guy named Joe Salazar

For some reason
he really liked me
and he showed it by
polishing my boots for me

Shined them every day
two pairs a day
and I'm here to tell you
he was the best

Still not exactly sure why that
was what he wanted to do
but he did it every day
for three months

I had nothing to give him in return
back then except friendship
and I have nothing more
now except for this

Almost fifty years later and
I have never forgotten his name

PAY CHECK

Pay check -$ 77

sent home –35
heels on boots – 3
new hat – 2
new gloves – 4
loans payed back –14
laundry – 2
personal hygiene –3

Left for the month - 14

GUARD DUTY

One time at Fort Gordon
I was on guard duty
It was kind of a pretend guard duty
where I spent two hours
just walking around a small PX
sort of a military convenience store
It was like from midnight till two
The store was closed no one around
but it was a very cold and icy day
At one point as I stepped forward
my front foot slid on the ice and I
began to fall
I instinctively threw out my hands
I had a nightstick but my
hand was through the thong
As I hit the ground the stick
swung up and whacked me in the eye
When they came to pick me up an hour later
A guy said, man what happened to your eye
I said nothing don't worry about it
We drove back to the barracks in silence

JOHN WAYNE

We keep hearing rumors
that they're currently filming
a John Wayne movie about Vietnam

Everyone's excited now about John Wayne
Everyone's excited now about going to Vietnam
Now it's a John Wayne war

"C. O."

At Fort Gordon Georgia
doing our advanced training
after Basic and it's Monday

One of the guys this morning
just put on civilian clothes and
refused to put on his uniform

He ignored a lawful order
from his squad leader and
platoon and personnel sergeants

and from the First Sergeant
and then a direct order from
the commanding officer

who he then cursed at
before being sent off
to see a psychiatrist

who said he wasn't insane
What he was was a college grad
who had volunteered for the army

but over Christmas leave
had changed his mind and is
now against the war in Vietnam

Which reminds me that two
other men are AWOL and haven't
come back from Christmas leave yet

ASSIGNMENT DAY

46 of us graduated
from our advanced training and
received our assignments today

1 stays here as an instructor
5 are being sent to Thailand
40 of us are going to Vietnam

That's an example of what they call the new math

19 The Smell of the Light

WALTER CRONKITE PULLS OUT

We have been too often disappointed
by the optimism of the American leaders
to have faith any longer in the
silver linings they find
in the darkest clouds

It seems now more certain than ever
that the bloody experience of Vietnam
is to end in a stalemate

To say that we are mired in stalemate
seems the only realistic
yet unsatisfactory conclusion

It is increasingly clear to this reporter
that the only rational way out
then will be to negotiate
Not as victors but as an
honorable people who
lived up to their pledge
to defend democracy
and did the best they could
And with those words
Walter Cronkite and
much of Middle America
pulled out of Vietnam

Just twenty-four days later
as if walking against a great wind
I would step off a plane and into
the heat and noise and bustle
of the Tan Son Nhut Air Base

OFF TO WAR

Standing by the plane
as we said goodbye
We hugged and
looked each other
in the eye

A mom and dad
a boy by their side
We chuckled
and laughed
with grins a mile wide

But the truth was something
we tried to hide
My mom kissed my cheek
but it was my dad
who cried

CLEANED OUT

I was in San Francisco
waiting to fly to Vietnam
the next day

and it was payday
Got my pay, went off to shower
pants thrown over a chair

Mid-shower it hits me
I race back to my room
and everything's still there

except the cash

I realize I'm among
a group of guys that
I don't even know

and we're all going to
Vietnam tomorrow or
soon but still

You would think a guy's stuff
wouldn't be messed with
Hope when I get to Vietnam

I don't need any cash

23   The Smell of the Light

VIETNAM

PLANE LOAD OF PORNOGRAPHY

Believe it or not we
flew into Saigon on
a commercial airliner
stewardesses and all

A couple of hours
before landing
they kept making the
same announcements

Be ready to move because the plane
wouldn't be on the ground long
and leave any pornography that
we brought with us on the plane

Take no magazines or any
pictures of naked women
with you off the plane
put it all in the seat-back

Guys were looking through
magazines one last time and
passing them around before
stowing them in the back of the seat

We landed in the heat and began
to move out quickly while the
plane prepared to return to the sky
carrying a full load of pornography

VUNG TAU I (THE LUCKIEST GUY)

I was in Vietnam for about two weeks
waiting to learn where I would be assigned

Eventually a Spec 4
walked up to me and said

You're the luckiest guy in the world

You're going to Vung Tau
That's probably the safest place in Vietnam

It's an airbase
It's an in-country R&R site

They don't ever get hit, man
You're the luckiest guy on earth

VUNG TAU II (THE SAFEST PLACE)

Vung Tau was one of the
safest places to serve out
your time in Vietnam

A beautiful coastal city
now with an airbase it
had long been a popular

resort beach for French colonials
and wealthy Vietnamese
But it was a city

of both war and peace
An important and active military port
it was also the major

in-country R&R spot
for the army with
about eighty bars

many named for American cities
It was long rumored to also be a
rest and recreation site for the Viet Cong

ARMS ROOM

One of the first things I did
was report to the arms room
where I would have an M14 rifle
checked out to me

But it would stay there
unless I needed it
That was two important
pieces of information

The fact that I was getting an
M14 instead of the newer M16
implied that I probably wouldn't
have to use it as much as someone
given an M16 somewhere else

It was also very telling that the weapon
would normally stay in the arms room
instead of me carrying it
This air base must be considered
a relatively safe place

There was another comforting moment
when I learned that the guy in charge of the
arms room was from Blackwell Oklahoma

I had just traveled more than 9,000 miles
and one of the first people I meet is a man
whose hometown is just 18 miles from mine

CHINOOKS

Our helicopters were called Chinooks
twin engine tandem rotor used for
moving troops placing artillery
and resupplying the battlefield

* * * *

Named for the indigenous people
of the American Pacific Northwest
with their shamans
and their long houses
once flattening the heads
of their children

* * * *

It was noted for not only being
among the heaviest lifting
but also for being one of the
fastest of all the helicopters

THE WORST, MAN!

The two guys who were chosen
to show me around the
company and the airfield

were both originally in an
infantry unit in Vietnam

They had voluntarily extended
their time in-country by six months

in exchange for getting stationed in a
safer place, the Vung Tau army airfield

They had been motivated in part by
the loss of a good friend in combat

But that's not the worst thing,
one of them said to me

Yeah said his buddy
When he died he was still a virgin
That's the worst, Man!

TWO (ARMY) OFFICERS/TWO (BAR) GIRLS

When I first got to Vung Tau

they were still talking about
an incident that had occurred
just a few months earlier
Two army officers who were

on base for temporary duty
believed they had been
ripped off by two bar girls
They had spent a lot of money

drinking with them and
became upset when the girls
demanded additional money before
they would have sex with them

They were very drunk when
they returned to their quarters
got a fragmentation grenade
from their equipment and

threw it on the bar's porch
where it blew out a four-foot
hole in the front wall
No one was injured but the

two officers were returned
to their original companies
where they were confined to
their quarters for ten months

and would never be given
another combat assignment

As related by Joseph W. Callaway, Jr. in *Mekong First Light*.

BEER ALCHEMY

What the hell is in this Vietnamese beer?
Formaldehyde, like they say?
Chunks of rice, as they say?
Ba Moui Ba Biere "33"
Is this the one guys call "tiger piss"
or does that honor go to
another Vietnamese beer?

HOOCH MAIDS

Hooch maids
Don't go to war without them
You leave each morning
to report for duty
leaving behind your
dirty clothes and boots
Returning to your bunk at
the end of your shift you note
that the hooch has been swept
your clothes are washed and folded
and your boots have been nicely shined
You hardly ever see her but
every day you note her work
She's a very important cog
behind our efforts to win the war

I SHALL NOT SEEK ...

My fellow Americans
I want to speak to you of peace
in Vietnam and Southeast Asia
No other question so
preoccupies our people

The offer I made public
in San Antonio was that
the United States would stop its
bombardment of North Vietnam
when that would lead promptly
to productive discussion

Hanoi denounced the offer
While their attack
during the Tet holidays did not
collapse the elected government of
South Vietnam as the Communists had hoped
it did cause widespread disruption and suffering

They are trying to make 1968 the
year of decision in South Vietnam
A year that brings a turning point in the struggle
This much is clear
If they mount another round of heavy attacks
they will not succeed in destroying South Vietnam
but tragically many men on both sides will be lost
There is no need for this to be so
There is no need to delay talks
Tonight I renew the offer to stop
the bombardment of North Vietnam
We ask that serious talks begin promptly

Tonight I am taking the first step
to deescalate the conflict by
substantially and unilaterally
reducing the present levels of hostilities

We are stopping aircraft attacks
on the principal populated areas and
food-producing areas of North Vietnam
Our purpose in this action is to reduce
the level of violence that now exists
Our restraint should be
matched by restraint in Hanoi
I call upon President Ho Chi Minh
to respond positively and favorably
to this new step toward peace

It is our fervent hope that North Vietnam
will now cease its efforts to
achieve a military victory and join
with us in moving toward the peace table
We are prepared to withdraw our forces
from South Vietnam as the other side
withdraws its forces to the north

One day my fellow citizens
there will be peace in Southeast Asia
and it will come because Asians were
willing to work sacrifice and
die by the thousands for it

But let it never be forgotten
that peace will also come because
America sent her sons to help secure it

37 The Smell of the Light

Finally my fellow Americans
Let me say this

There is division in the American house tonight
I cannot disregard the peril to the
progress of the American people and the
hope and prospect of peace for all people
I would ask all Americans
to guard against divisiveness
I have concluded that
I should not permit the presidency
to become involved in partisan divisions
that are developing in this political year

With America's sons in the fields far away
America's future under challenge at home
and our hopes and the world's hopes
for peace in the balance every day
I do not believe that I should devote my
time to any personal partisan causes or to
any duties other than that of the presidency

Accordingly I shall not seek
and I will not accept the
nomination of my party for another
term as your president

Good night and God bless all of you

President Lyndon Baines Johnson
March 31, 1968

APRIL FOOL'S

It was a Monday morning
not that days of the week
really mattered

Anderson came to the door
of the hooch
Did you hear?

It's over
It's all over
We're goin' home

He stuck his hand out to me

I saw my girl
my mom
my dog and home

I reached out to shake his hand

"April Fool's!" he said
and kind of chucked
me on the shoulder

Now I like a good joke
as much as the next man but
I don't do April Fool's anymore

LEPROSARIUM

One day we donated 12 barrels
of diesel fuel to a leprosarium
northeast of Bien Hoa
There are men and women who
are still willing to take great risks
in order to serve others

THE DISAPPEARING FACE

I've just been here a month but
Don has been over here six months

and he says he's concerned because
when he thinks about his girlfriend

he can't recall what she looks like
He can't bring her into his mind

TORTOISE

There are four sacred animals
in the Vietnamese culture

Dragon
Phoenix
Tortoise
Unicorn

I'll give you one guess as to
which one I saw while I was there

EATING GLASS

The first time I saw
a preschool kid
(Do they have schools here?)
smoking a cigarette I
just stood and stared

Mama-sans squatting
to pee along the road
never drew a second glance
But a child casually smoking
was hard for me to unsee

For a month I had a
reoccurring dream of
a smoking toddler a
circus performer eating glass
and a ward filled with

Thalidomide babies
But after about
four weeks the dream
became a memory of
a dream of a memory

HILLCLIMBER 027

On May 4 Hillclimber 027
performed one of the fastest
air rescues of the entire war
Major Degner and Warrant Officer Taylor
were bringing the ship back to Vung Tau
when Specialist Choate the flight engineer
saw a crashed USAF 0-1 directly below them
They entered a descent and landed near the crash
Crewmembers set off to assist the pilots
Neither were seriously injured and
were loaded on 027 to Vung Tau where
an ambulance would be standing by
Total time from crash to hospital
was 31 minutes

JUNE 2, 1968

Rain
all
day
rain
all
day
rain
all
day
rain
all
day
rain
all
day

BOBBY KENNEDY

I was in Vietnam when
I heard on the radio
that Bobby Kennedy had
died from his wounds

I had read everything
I could get my hands
on about him and
had become a big fan

It was a very sad day
There were as many tears
in Vietnam as anywhere
else in the world

And I wasn't sure
I wanted to come home

DARKER THAN AMBER

My favorite reading material
that my mom sent me were
the Travis McGee novels
by John D. MacDonald

One of our pilots, a major
always insisted that I pass them
on to him when I was through
My favorite was *Darker Than Amber*

The movie version later made of it
was the very first film I watched
when I got out of the army and
it gave me a sense that I was

reconnecting with the world
but it also led me to recall when
and where I read it and to
remember that brave major

DYLAN WINS THE WAR

From a prompt by D.C.

I had a dream that
Bob Dylan spent his
months of seclusion
after his famous accident
fighting in Vietnam

In the dream I
saw him and he was
in uniform wearing
pearl-handled revolvers
Patton style

But all of his insignia
were upside down
When I asked someone
about it they said
Well, that's Bob

As he walked away he
turned back to me and said
You can either sing this war
to an end or you
can fight it to one

NUMBERS

Officials have just announced
that more Americans were killed
during the first six months of 1968
than in all of 1967

So next year we could
match that yearly number
in just the first three
months of the year

And I'll still be here
during that time
considering a mathematical computation
that is rapidly closing in on itself

FIGHTING FIRE

In July some of our helicopters
were involved in the first
extensive experimentation with
airborne fire-fighting techniques
using a 450-gallon bucket
Nice to know our combat training
would soon lead to civilian agencies
being better able to combat wildfires

OH, THE HUMANITY!
(From a letter home.)

A Chinook
from another company
disintegrated   in midair
last week and
all on board were killed
It is still unexplained

HOME FRONT

The walls of our hooches
were plastered with
pictures from magazines
of naked women
bush and all
But not just any women
Mainly young slender
big-breasted
California-bronzed
women who were
always looking at us
as if they clearly
understood what
we were fighting for

27 HITS

On July 22 Hillclimber 024
(Pilots: Warrant Officers Martin and Milsson)
received 27 hits from Viet Cong
Shot away the #1 hydraulics and
fumes from a fuel leak filled the ship
They landed in a secure area
crewmembers made necessary repairs
and four hours later they were up and away

SOMETIMES YOU JUST CAN'T CATCH A BREAK

While piloting Hillclimber 027
Warrant Officer Boschma
was wounded in the left arm
by sniper fire
Warrant Officer Nicol took over
the controls while
Specialist Harrington
administered first aid
The mission continued but
when they returned home the
flight crewmembers began
razzing the injured pilot for getting
blood on his seat and the console

BETTY AND VERONICA

My buddy and I decided
to go into Vung Tau
to a local bar for a
little female activity

The woman who ran the place
pointed to three other women
I chose one but my buddy saw
a girl no more than twelve
sitting in a corner by herself
reading a comic book
He asked if she was available
and the mama-san nodded yes
The girl put down her comic

****

I later asked my buddy
if he had thought that
was the right thing to do
He said what do you mean

I said you don't feel bad
about what you did
He said no besides she gave him the clap
I said maybe we ought to slow down some
He said not a chance
that's why God made penicillin

I never went back there with
him again but he went back
and I went back

HOW'S YOUR VD LATELY?
(A public service announcement played over Armed Forces Radio Vietnam)

Question: How's your VD lately?

No we're not speaking about your
vicious dog or your vitamin deficiency
We're talking about a very personal problem

The man to see is the medic

Once you see him
your world will once again
be a very happy place

A BALL OF FLAMES

Numerous hits from VC snipers
brought Hillclimber 989 to the
ground in a ball of flames
They had just departed a fire support base
when they were hit
With their aft end on fire the
load was jettisoned and the
ship put into autorotation
After a soft landing the crew
ran from the ship as
the aft pylon fell off
Another of our ships
(Magel and Adams) landed
and picked up the men and
the two crews returned home

PRUESS

One of my buddies
CWO R.J. Pruess took a
round in the leg while
flying Hillclimber 074

It wasn't too serious but
bad enough to mean he's
not coming back here
I probably won't see him again

* * * *

He always liked looking at pictures
I had of my girlfriend and we
shared recommendations of our
favorite Harold Robbins novels

* * * *

He wrote me about five
weeks after the incident
saying he was back
to walking normally

But the entrance hole
still hadn't healed shut so
he'd be going on convalescent
leave for about two months
His biggest hope was to be back
in Vietnam by January and that he
wasn't sure he could return to the 147th
but that he sure planned to try like hell

CALLED HOME BY DEATH

In these crazy times
you just never know
from which direction
it's going to come

The man who works nights
in the orderly room
has the job of making
early morning wake-up calls
He's woke me up
every morning at 4:30
every day that I've worked
the past two months

Yesterday he was notified
by the Red Cross that
his father had been killed
in an automobile accident

* * * *

That's the word they used
automobile four syllables
You can't just say car and be done?
You have to drag it out?

* * * *

He's almost home now
called there by death
and will soon return
to this place of war

EIGHT ROUNDS

One of our aircraft
working up north of Saigon
was hit today by eight rounds

4 struck the blades
2 went into the cockpit
2 into the main body of the ship

One of our aircraft
was hit today by eight rounds
But who's counting?

NOT WITHOUT A HITCH

One of our ships dropped
ninety very large flares in
support of a search mission
for a downed Mohawk plane

While preparing to drop
one of the last flares a
crewmember thought he
had forgotten to trigger it

so he pulled it back
into the aircraft
and it exploded also
setting two others off

The entire helicopter
could have easily been lost
but the flight engineer
picked up the three flares

and threw them out of
the tail end of the ship
One man was badly burned with
fragment wounds in the head

SEATS

Our Chinook helicopters
were allowed to carry 33
Americans and their
gear in one load

Because that's how
many seats we had
Everyone had
to be in a seat

When we carried
South Vietnamese soldiers
we could usually take 55
Some had seats

One time we carried
little Vietnamese children
and got 93 of them in
Most not in seats

Those kids had the
time of their life
The time of
their life

SHIT

There are only two times I can
remember getting the shit detail
and only in the military does that
phrase mean exactly what it says

Tim spoke of "the honor" of the assignment
but I don't think he was serious
So while we low-level guys
were stirring the shit literally

it was also being done figuratively
by the Viet Cong, Saigon, Hanoi
and in Washington D.C.
There was plenty of shit to go around

LONESOME CITIES

Today's mail brought a book
of poems from Rod McKuen
Lonesome Cities
Inside of it he wrote

Billy –
Stay well
Rod McKuen
6 Sept 68

I consider it to be my
own personal poem
written to me
by Rod McKuen

"CRAZY RALPH"
This is based on a letter I wrote to my mom from
Vietnam on September 30, 1968.

We had a guy in our hooch
that was something else
His name was Ralph

Funny to be with and
funny to listen to

His first ten months in Vietnam he'd been
busted from Specialist Fourth Class
to private, fined $150
and had been given
28 days of extra duty

He wasn't a bad guy
he just didn't like the army
He got drunk all the time
but was never a hostile drunk

Once he was too drunk
to go on guard duty so
they fined him and
gave him extra duty

Another time he took a truck
from the motor pool
and five cases of fruit
and was caught going into
the South Vietnamese Army's
women's compound with
all kinds of wild ideas

65   The Smell of the Light

The 54th Aviation Company
was right next to us and
they had a pet duck

The duck wandered into
our area one day and
Ralph and another guy
caught it chopped off its head
plucked it and it ended up in
our mess hall's refrigerator

Ralph says he loves to eat duck!
Crazy Ralph

YOUNG AND DISTANT LOVE

Tim was my roommate
in our hooch on the
airfield at Vung Tau
With three months left he
put in a request for duty
when he leaves Vietnam

He requested Ft. Rucker
in Alabama because his
girlfriend lived less than a
hundred miles from there
I saw several pictures of
her and she was beautiful

Well, out of twenty guys
who put in their requests
at about the same time he
was the only one to get
the place he asked for

Then two days later he
received a letter from her
saying her father had been
transferred and they were
now living in California

A few weeks after that
another letter from her said
she wanted to join the navy
so she could be close to him

Nice reason but wrong idea

67 The Smell of the Light

He wrote back to tell her not to
hoping that she didn't sign up
on the spur of the moment

THE TALL MAN

I was sitting in a restaurant in
a big hotel right on the coast
eating the biggest freshest
shrimp I had ever seen

listening to a Filipino rock band
singing in a speeded-up manner
If you're going to San Francisco
be sure to wear some flowers in your hair

when I saw three MPs chasing the
tallest man I had ever seen in a uniform
He had no flowers in his hair so I had a
pretty good idea where he wasn't going

MOCKINGBIRD

When I was told I was
being promoted I was
also told I'd be going to
Dong Tam to make it official
and would stay there overnight
That evening they dropped
a couple of white sheets
down the side of a shed
because it was their
regular movie night
The film we watched was
To Kill a Mockingbird
A timeless movie that would
become a beloved classic
I watched it that night
under the skies of Vietnam
While Scout and Jem grew up
over a couple of years I was
moving up the military ranks
None of us were as innocent
as we once had been

DREAM

Her bouncing bettys
were barely contained
in her flowery halter-top

She walked so fast her
peace symbol swung
in a crazy 270° arc

My year is half over
this dream is winding down
and the light from the dawn

has a smell all its own
Not the air never the air
but the light

MESSAGE FROM MILO

I had a token bet
of just one dollar
with Lieutenant Mong

on the Oklahoma and
Notre Dame game
I lost the bet and

when I got to work
the next morning
someone had written

on the board
"Okies can't play
football, McCloud"

I don't have
any proof but
I think it was

put there by
Warrant Officer Milo
And what he wrote

contained a terrible slur
Okies can too
play football!

OFFICERS' CLUB

I was never an officer but
my job in flight operations
meant I worked with them
all day long

So a few times one or
another of the pilots
would invite me to hang
out at the Officers' Club

The most memorable time
was a movie night and
they were all excited and
looking forward to watching

Those Magnificent Men in Their Flying Machines
A 1965 movie about a
fictional 1910 air race
from London to Paris

Watched in 1968 by a
truly daring group of pilots and I've often
wondered what each of them dreamed
when they fell asleep that night

CONVERSION DAY (C-DAY)

We were not allowed to
have actual American money
while stationed in-country

Our currency was in the form of
military payment certificates
called MPCs

It was illegal for
Vietnamese to possess them
but they were greatly valued

and would end up in the black market
amid great concern that they
would harm the local economy

So one day totally by surprise
we were restricted to base and
all our MPCs were exchanged

for new ones with a different look
meaning all of the previous
ones had no value at all

I can still see the Vietnamese faces
outside the fence begging and pleading
for us to exchange what they had for them

No can do we told them as they looked
at fists full of now worthless paper
No can do

GUN MEN

I spent a lot of time
around M14s and M16s
and often wore a .45

But I wasn't no gun man
A couple of guys in our
company were though

Once I walked up on
them while they were
arguing I mean arguing

over Wyatt Earp's Buntline
Special revolver about
whether the length of the

barrel was 12" or just 10"
I guess you could say they
were academic gun men

SYDNEY, AUSTRALIA

I went on R&R to
Sydney Australia and greatly
disappointed my grandma

Now I didn't do it
on purpose but the
rest of her life she
never got over the fact
that I spent seven days on
the continent of Australia
and did not see one kangaroo

Ladies and gentlemen of the jury
I state my case
I was nineteen years old
had been in Vietnam
and away from home
for over seven months

When I first landed in Sydney
and after getting briefed on
what to plan on doing and
what to avoid for seven days

I headed straight for the
King's Cross entertainment section
found the Whiskey a Go Go and
made it my temporary headquarters

In closing I can honestly admit
that I got pulled into the crowded
sparkly glorious city and fell in

with a bohemian crowd

Never once did I give a second's
thought to go looking for a kangaroo

RUBBER SOUL

About every other evening
if the movie is no good
Vaughn brings his guitar into
my hooch and we sing Beatles
Dylan and Simon & Garfunkel

He has a guitar that
he's just learned to play
since he's been in Vietnam
He plays very well besides
having a really great voice

I can back him up OK I'd say but
when it comes to a solo part
there's no question he is better
We both love the early Beatles songs
especially anything on Rubber Soul

ROOM 6

They called her "Room 6"
That was also her base of operations
One room in a downtown hotel
Room 6
She only provided one service for GIs
but it was a popular one
You might say she was a specialist
You entered and paid her
She would always open and hand you
a cold bottle of Coca-Cola
and then she'd begin

* * * *

Her waiting room was usually full but
there were always magazines to look at

* * * *

She worked seven days a week
Even worked after being beaten by a client
A bad black man she said
A very bad black man

WRITE YOUR MOM (THE BLUE PERIOD)

One time I was called into
the First Sergeant's office
and ripped up one side
and down the other

For some reason I had
found myself in a depressed
period and had not written
a letter to my mother
in over a month

Turns out she had written
the company commander
to make sure I was all right
He didn't like receiving that letter
and told the First Sergeant to
make sure he never got
another one from her

First Sergeant bawled me out
in no uncertain terms and
told me that the rest of my
time in Vietnam I was to have
at least one letter addressed
to my mother on top of his
desk every Monday morning
I wrote my mother that I had
gone through a period where I
was very depressed and told her
I called it my "blue period" and
that I felt as alone as if I was
on the dark side of the moon

THANKSGIVING MESSAGE
(Anonymous, from our Thanksgiving menu, 1968)

The necessity for keeping the defenses
of our nation strong and alert has
placed you a long way from home
on a holiday that is traditionally
a family affair

Your family along with millions
of other Americans will thank God
this day that you protect our country
Thanksgiving is an American holiday and you
are celebrating it in the finest possible way

RAT FINK

Somebody got their hands on
some real grainy black and white
porno the old school stuff
They charged a small amount
turned out all the lights and

started up the projector
I still remember one of the scenes
but it would serve no purpose
in having it described here
Anyhow after a few weeks the

whole operation got shut down
One of our own had squealed
The rest of my time there we
played a mental game in which
we tried to determine just

who among us would
have stooped that low
We never figured it out but
it gave us something to
do to help pass the time

HIS SISTER

One of the guys
was really proud
of his sister

After all
she'd been in D.C.
with Abbie Hoffman

when he had
levitated the Pentagon
Put that he said

put that
in your pipe
and smoke it

SHORT

These are the various stages of my countdown for going home that I kept on a short-timer's calendar.

Half-way through: 182 days left
Under 100: 99 days left
One month: 30 days left
Stopped flying on any missions: 14 days left
Single digit: 9 days left
HOME!

LET'S FIGHT

A guy in our barracks
absolutely hated me
One of those no reason just
personality conflict things

Once he caught me alone
and said let's fight
I said what?
What for?

He said look I
don't like you
and you don't like me
So here's the deal

I've been like this with
other guys and we'd just
have a fist fight and then
everything would be okay

I said you're crazy
He shoved me and said
come on let's do it
Come on

I said no chance
That's crazy
I'm not gonna fight you
No way

I never fought him for three reasons
I couldn't see anything behind his eyes

85 The Smell of the Light

It wouldn't have proved anything
And I sure wasn't going to give him the satisfaction

BAR (WAR?) WOUND

I was at a bar I had been
to several times before
talking to a bar girl
that I had spoken
with a few times
Things were relaxed

All of a sudden
there was this flash
of miscommunication
She lashed out and sank
her teeth into my bicep
went in tight and locked up

I have no idea what
she thought I'd said
but it drove her crazy

Took two other guys
pulling back on her forehead
to get her teeth out of my skin
Went straight to the medic
Got a tetanus shot
Doc said it was a pretty unusual injury

I went back two weeks later
the girl badly beaten avoided me
When I asked another girl about it
she said mama-san had done it to the girl
since what the girl had done to me
would be bad for business

MIDAIR ACCIDENT

The other day
one of our aircraft
was taking off from

the Can Tho airport
when it lost power
and

started

coming

down

hit some large cable wires
lost the rotor blades in flight
and landed upside down

in a rice paddy
Five Vietnamese were killed
twenty-one injured

As for the crew there was
just one sprained back
The pilots were two

of my favorites so
I was very happy it
turned out the way it did

COMMANDER'S CHRISTMAS MESSAGE

(From our Christmas menu, 1968)

Christmas has a special meaning
for American soldiers in Vietnam
Amid the tragedy and ugliness of war
the Holy Season reminds us
of the joy and beauty of peace

We who serve in this distant
land may be justly proud
No finer gift may one provide than
to give of his own that his brother
might share what he himself enjoys

This is what we are doing as we
assist in supporting the Vietnamese in
their struggle to maintain independence
As we face a coming new year may we pray
for success in our mission and peace on earth

Creighton W. Abrams
General, United States Army
Commanding

A CHRISTMAS PRAYER
(From our Christmas menu, 1968)

Heavenly Father
We thank Thee
for invading history
that we might for

all time understand
the intensity of Thy
love for us
Make of us modern

wise men who dare
to serve Thee from
the heat of Vietnam
Grant that as we

celebrate Thy Nativity
our lives shall radiate
Thy love humility
and selflessness

Gerard J. Gefell
Chaplain (Col) USA
Staff Chaplain

ANN-MARGRET

Saw the Bob Hope show
Dong Tam 1968
30,000 in attendance
I was third row center
Bob Hope, Ann-Margret, Miss World
and a cast of about twenty
I happened to catch her
as I was leaving
Signed a photo and
shook my hand
She said, "Please forgive me
for perspiring. A woman
should never perspire, she
should always glow."
As she was being driven away
she said, "I hope I get
to see you when
you come home."

APOLLO 8

Three men just went
around the moon
first time ever

Their TV broadcast
this Christmas Eve
was most watched ever

First time that Time
chose three people
as Men of the Year

Dave wants to R&R
on the moon saying there's
a first time for everything

WEATHER IN HELL

The entire month of December 1968
every day saw a warmer than average temperature
every single day in fact 33 days in a row
of warmer than average temperatures

Looks like the war is heating up
Looks like we're moving closer to hell

WORKER BEES AND FLIES

Thomas threw down
the *Reader's Digest*

Says here he said
the worker bee lives
just one year

So my time in Vietnam
would be like his whole life
It just seems like my whole life

But a fly only lives two weeks
Two weeks, man
They don't ever get to be short

Negative, said Jimmy P
picking up the *Reader's Digest*

Negative, man
That's not how I see it
I say they're always short

TRIP TO TOWN

One of our pilots
was jumped by two
Vietnamese civilians
when he went into town
They asked for his billfold
He politely refused and

they proceeded to pounce
One had a club
the other a knife
He held his own
for a few minutes

then broke away
An MP took him to the
hospital x-rayed for
skull fracture all was OK
He did have three knife cuts
on his face not deep

Word went around
and this set kind of a
standard for us that we
were never to give in
to punks like these

SARAH LAWRENCE

Getting ready to lift off
from Dong Tam
he made sure the Army nurse
was buckled in
hooked up

He said You doin' okay?
She said:
I wanted to go to Sarah Lawrence
He said hang on
just hang on
She said:
I wanted to go to Sarah Lawrence

He said I heard
you did all that you could
That no one
could have done more
She said:
I wanted to go to Sarah Lawrence
I should've gone to Sarah Lawrence

RADIO ADVENTURE

I was monitoring the radio
one evening when a voice came
on the emergency frequency

He said he was in a two-man LOH
the pilot had been wounded
and was unconscious and he was
at the controls of a helicopter
for the first time in his life

He requested instructions from
someone so he could land the ship

He was heard by a pilot
flying in the area who started
giving him instructions as to
what to do with his hands and feet
until he made a perfect landing
It all lasted for about thirty
minutes and I heard both
sides of the conversation
the entire time

A thrilling radio adventure
only this one had been real

WOUNDS

No Purple Heart
but I was wounded
twice in Vietnam

Once when I was
hit in the head
with a rock
thrown by a young boy

And once when I was
bitten severely
on the bicep
by a bar girl

I was wounded
twice in Vietnam
No Purple Heart

WAR (THE LONGEST DAY)

My regular job didn't include flying
but I often went up in the air
during some of my time off
We were usually just involved in support
but the ship I was on January 5

got 15 ½ hours in the air
5 ½ hours was night combat assault
We were resupplying a front-line unit
in direct contact and fighting
with the enemy at the time

We flew right against known enemy positions
carrying seven loads in receiving
heavy enemy fire but no hits
We were resupplying a 9th Infantry Division
Company that had a VC company pinned down

that in turn had another U.S. company pinned down
We left at 8:15 in the morning
returning at 1:30 the next morning
covering the entire IV Corps area of South Vietnam and
once being less than ten miles from the Cambodian
border

TRAGEDY ON THE AIRFIELD
(The Day We Lost Weldon Hodges of Midland, TX)

This morning about 1:00
one of our guys from Texas
was performing some routine
night maintenance on

Hillclimber 128
He was lying on top of the
aircraft checking for an
oil leak ship running when

for some unknown reason he
raised right up into one of
the forward blades and was
knocked to the ground

There was no blood
pronounced DOA at hospital
He was going home in a
little over three months

That's kind of how we describe
people around here
Who they are is sometimes only
how long they have left in Vietnam

ROCKETS

Both times the airfield was
hit with Russian-made
rockets I was on duty

Loudest noise I've ever heard
A cracking sound like the
universe breaking apart

Both times I immediately
went under the desk
wondering how long

If you ask me what those rockets
looked like I'd say the underside
of a company desk

LAST TWO WEEKS (THE CHANT)

There was an unwritten rule
in our helicopter company
that when down to two
weeks left in Vietnam you
did not fly on any missions

Didn't want to lose anyone
that close to going home
So that became our goal
That blessed two week point
Get there and let the

chant begin I
can't fly I
can't fly I

A STORY I NEVER ENJOY TELLING

I had one regular bar
in town that became
my favorite the

papa-san liked me
and let me charge beers
toward the end of

each month or so
He just kept my
Seiko watch until

I paid him off
each time
After a few months he

began to just
trust me and stopped
keeping my watch but

he didn't know how
long I had left
and I was able to

skip out of there
owing him more than
a hundred bucks which

means I did my own
individual part to
screw the Vietnamese just

103 The Smell of the Light

as they had been
being screwed on an
international scale for decades

DISTINCTION

About two and a half million men
served in Vietnam during the war
I don't know how many of them my buddy knew
but he once told me that I was the only guy
he ever knew who served in Vietnam
that did not get a suntan

105 The Smell of the Light

MY VIETNAM EXPERIENCE

I landed in Vietnam

Martin Luther King, Jr. was assassinated
Senator Robert F. Kennedy was assassinated
There was rioting at the Democratic National Convention in Chicago
Students took over the administrative offices at Columbia University
Catholic activists burned hundreds of files from a draft board in Maryland

I left Vietnam

IN THE ARMY, BUT AFTER VIETNAM

THE SAINT CHRISTOPHER MEDAL (A LOVE STORY)

The day before I left for 'Nam
my mom's best friend Anne
gave me a Saint Christopher medal
She asked me to put it on right then
and to never take it off
If nothing else do it for me.

The patron saint of travelers he
also holds the patronage of soldiers
I put it around my neck

My time in Vietnam didn't
involve the constant danger
that so many men faced but
there was flying and mortars
and twice there had been
those Russian-made rockets

And hell
if nothing else
I was in Vietnam

The first day home I showed
Anne and my mom that I
was still wearing the medal
I had never taken it off
That night I went to sleep
with it around my neck
When I woke up in the morning
it was gone so I searched for it
It was never found it had done its job

BACK IN THE WORLD

Hey soldier how you doin'
Can I buy you a beer
Is it as bad over there as they say
You think we're ever gonna finish that war

Hey soldier need a ride?
My cousin from Chicago was over there
You think you might have known him?
Did you shoot anyone

Hey soldier I hope you know
I took good care of your girlfriend
while you were over there
Your folks doin' OK?

Hey soldier you look different somehow
You think you're gonna stay in the army?
Let me buy you a beer
I heard it was pretty bad over there

BEER

When I got home from Vietnam
I wanted a beer

Not an easy thing to get if you're a
boy under twenty-one in Oklahoma

So I got one of the Coffman boys
either Jack or Mike I don't remember

And he Jack or Mike bought
me a six-pack of cold beer

Just home from Vietnam
I had some thinking to do

I wanted to drink beer while doing it and
was very lucky to run into Jack or Mike

When a young man's head is full
of memories thoughts and ideas

instead of just sitting in a library he may
want to take some beer down a country road

Not an easy thing to do if you're a
boy under twenty-one in Oklahoma

SLEEP

My first month home after Vietnam
I could sleep as much as I liked
No one was brave enough to wake me
because they had all heard about
the startle reflex of a war vet
I don't remember ever being startled
but I sure got a lot of good sleep

POT (THE DISAPPOINTMENT)

I'm pretty sure the statute
of limitation has run out
so yes I have smoked pot
twice both times in the army

But not in Vietnam
And it never did anything for me

I've always been disappointed
that I never got anything out of it
just as many have been disappointed
that I never smoked pot in Vietnam

DARK SIDE OF THE MOON

In a letter home
to my mom once
I told her I was so
lonely it must have
been like being on the
dark side of the moon

Just a few months later
Armstrong and Collins
walked on the moon
Maybe not on the dark side
but they failed to report
any sightings of Viet Cong

I think by that time we
had them pretty well
rounded up and controlled
Either that or they had
already been taken out
by Jules Verne

TRANQUILITY BASE

We watched the TV coverage
of the first time that men
walked on the moon
with the same sense of awe
as virtually everyone else

In our company's dayroom
next to the airfield at Fort Riley
we watched for hours as
the empty Schlitz cans were
added to the stack in front of us

The greatest technological achievement
in the history of mankind
and we wanted to make sure
that our efforts matched what
we were watching on TV

So we piled the cans high
By now we were experts at this
and we fully understood the
human accomplishment
playing out in front of us

and we piled the cans high
That night we went to bed with a
tremendous sense of fulfillment because we
had established a company record for the
number of empty beer cans formed in one stack

MY LAI

Only eight days before
I first set foot in Vietnam
American troops murdered
more than 400 unarmed
South Vietnamese civilians

Men women children infants
gang-raped and mutilated
The massacre took place
in the hamlets of
My Lai and My Khe
in the Son My village
in Quang Ngai Province

The My Lai Massacre or
Massacre at Son My or
The Pinkville Massacre

I found out about it
when the rest of the world did
eight months after I left Vietnam
It had been there
hanging in the air
the entire time I was in-country
but I didn't know didn't know
Once I found out
I wasn't surprised wasn't surprised

McTEAGUE

An army buddy in Kansas
seemed extremely literate
He kept reading his
favorite book, McTeague
over and over again

He especially liked the part
where the dentist
bit his wife's fingers
so severely that it
led to amputation

* * * *

He would build
plastic models of
flying machines
with exacting precision
and a great sense of love

He spent many hours
putting together three
pretty good-sized
army helicopters
of different kinds

I walked into the dayroom
once and he said watch this
He then set fire to each of
them and we stood together
watching them melt

He said that was something
wasn't it?
I think I shrugged
He scooped up the mess
and said let's go eat

SLOW MOTION

Once I put my fist
through a window
for no reason at all and
watched the glass breaking
in slow motion

OUT OF THE ARMY

AIR MEDAL

The only medal I
received during the war
other than routine ones
was an Air Medal

"25 aerial missions over hostile territory"

I got it in 1969 and in
1985 I placed it inside my
dad's coffin just before
they closed the lid

My mom had wanted me to
come home with all her heart
So had my dad but I think he
also wanted me to be brave

The medal always meant
more to him than anyone else
so I let him take it with him
along with my love

PLATOON (EVERYONE'S VIETNAM IS DIFFERENT)

In early 1987 I took my mom
to see the movie Platoon
I couldn't relate to it
any more than she could
It was not my Vietnam War
I hadn't been a grunt
trudging through jungles
fighting my own buddies one day
and the Viet Cong the next
There was not one Vietnam War
When did you go?
Where were you stationed?
What was your job?
I couldn't relate to Platoon
any more than my mother could
But Good Morning Vietnam
Now that was a different story

HER SON

Today I talked to a Gold Star
Mother Irene Faught
Her son Frank was killed
in Vietnam the month
before I got there

It's been almost 20 years now
but she said just the other day
she heard a man who had
called in to a local radio show say
Everybody knows that only the
scum went to Vietnam

She said My son was not scum!
He was drafted and as a loyal and patriotic
man believed he should serve his country
She said you tell them you tell them
My boy was not scum

AT THE WALL

It was me
in the rain
at night
in the rain
at the Wall
in the rain

No school kids
no volunteers
just me and
58,000 stories
and all I remember
is the rain

127 The Smell of the Light

TODAY

VUNG TAU III (TODAY)

Wayne writes to tell me that he's
recently been back to Vung Tau
and he says it's beautiful
It is still beautiful

Except the beaches are
polluted with globs of oil
from the Russian oil rigs
in the ocean

As for the town itself where
we drank and fought and loved
it's now obscenely crowded
with drunken Russians

And so this battle in the
old Cold War is over and
to the victor go
the spoiled spoils

DISABILITY

The VA considers my Type 2 Diabetes
to be a service-connected disability
Diabetes is so closely linked
to Agent Orange that if
you're diabetic and served
at least one day in-country it's
considered to have been the cause
You don't have to prove any connection
You just have to have been there
One thing that most wars have in common
is that they all seem to keep on giving

LINH IS BORED

Linh is bored with
studying about this old war

She innocently flirts with
a boy across the room

She thinks about being anywhere
other than sitting at this long desk

looking out a window
deciphering the cloud shapes

in a room so crowded she
never has her own space

She knows tomorrow is her
day to help clean her school

But today she's bored
studying about this American war

at her desk in this room
that are all a part of this school

built on blood-soaked ground
in the city of Dien Bien Phu

ADDITIONAL POEMS

I did not start writing poetry until after the completion of my military service. These last two poems were the first ones I ever wrote. The year was 1971. They do not relate to any direct experience I had in the war. But they did come straight from my subconscious.

BLUE

As the rain fell it proved the sergeant was a liar
The cracking thunder mixed with the rifle fire
   The infant boy gropes at his father's hand

The vicious sound of war roars on
Already many good men are gone
   The relatives think the little man is grand

The returning patrol confirmed they were near
Covering his eyes was a thin film of fear
   The time has come, the boy starts school

His thoughts return to his home and his wife
He wonders again why he's risking his life
   If he learns anything he can't be called a fool

The leaders at home who are supporting this fight
What makes them think they are always right
   Education complete, his diploma he carries

There were so many things that weren't clear
But now the word is passed, the time is near
   His parents feel it's time he marries

He glances upward, the sky is black
He looks for God, no stars blink back
   His country is at war, he doesn't think it's right

When it comes he hopes to be ready
He is sure of nothing, his hand is unsteady
   But he's called to leave his home and join the fight

With a terrifying scream, they're finally rushing
From the corner of his eye he sees blood gushing
The cracking thunder mixed with the rifle fire

The time is here, his future dies
He drops his gun and closes his eyes
As the rain fell it proved the sergeant was a liar

AMERICA

Just before I killed him
I saw his eyes
pleading
Then blood was running between them
and he stumbled
and fell to his knees
and it was over
He lay on his back
and still his eyes were open
moist
I checked his pockets
and found only a snapshot
of a beautiful child
with shining eyes
A younger replica
of the man who lay before me
I dropped my gun
and replaced the photo
buttoning back the pocket
I sat beside the body
until Harper came up and said, "Let's go"
I said, "Go ahead
I'll follow"
but I knew I wouldn't
I began digging in the ground
and worked
and sweated more than an hour
then rolled the body into the hole
and followed it with my gun
I filled it back
and sat beneath a tree a few feet away

ACKNOWLEDGEMENTS

After decades of teaching, writing about, and talking about the Vietnam War I decided in 2015 that I had exhausted what I had to say, or at least what I wanted to say. I was through. But then my friend, Tim Bonea, made me aware that my book from 1989, *What Should We Tell Our Children About Vietnam?* (University of Oklahoma Press), was still being used regularly in both English and American history classes at the University School of Milwaukee, WI, one of the nation's leading private college preparatory schools.

Somehow the fact that two instructors, Dr. Laurie Walczak and Mr. Chuck Taft, were still using my materials, encouraged me to continue writing about Vietnam. I just moved in a different direction. When I first communicated with "Doc" and Chuck I had seven Vietnam poems. Within a few months I had more than a hundred. I sent a selection of the poems to them and they began using them with their classes and invited me to Skype with the students several times. I credit them with being the main inspiration for what developed into this book.

When this collection was about two-thirds complete I showed it to a good buddy, Jimmy Pollard, of Massachusetts, when he was on one of his visits to Tulsa. I had literally just pulled the collection together and we were in the front seat of my car with the hole-punch on the floor along with hundreds of small, round, punched-out pieces of paper all over the seats.

He read dozens of the poems and was very kind with his comments. His face lit up as he rapidly turned the pages. He repeated several of the lines aloud, kept nodding his head, and then actually thanked me for letting him read them. His reaction inspired me to get the thing finished.

Teresa Stites, who works at the Dick Conner Correctional Center in Hominy, Oklahoma, along with warden Janet Dowling, invited me to read my poems to the Veterans Club, made up of medium security prisoners. Jimmie Tramel, TULSA WORLD writer, learned I was going there and tagged along with me, with WORLD photographer Jessie Wardarski. He then wrote a great Sunday feature article about the experience.

Writer Teresa Miller encouraged me and suggested I contact Bill and Lara Bernhardt. The Bernhardts' interest in my work was immediate and long lasting. They wanted to produce this book from the first moment they read the poems. I want to thank Bill Bernhardt for his creative efforts in doing the editing of this book. A poet is truly blessed when they can have their work edited by another poet. A few of my poems are based on information written by LTC Paul E. Berg in the history section of the current 147th Hillclimber webpage.

I was encouraged along the way by several noted Vietnam veteran writers, including Wayne Karlin, Marc Leepson, Professor John Clark Pratt, David Willson, and W.D. Ehrhart.

Jamie Dotson helped me prepare the manuscript electronically so it could be submitted to the publisher.

I was especially blessed to have one of the world's greatest songwriters, Graham Nash, read and comment on these poems.

Finally, thanks to my biggest supporter, Kira Fell, whose enthusiasm for my work served to propel me further down the road, and to the person who has supported my work longer than anyone else, my sister, Shelley Waldo.

ABOUT THE AUTHOR

Bill McCloud has taught American history since 1974. He is a three-time Teacher of the Year. His book, *What Should We Tell Our Children About Vietnam?*, published by the University of Oklahoma Press, was a finalist for the Oklahoma Book Award. His Vietnam papers have been purchased by the Houghton Library at Harvard University. His Vietnam War poems are used as part of the curriculum in both English and American history classes at the University School of Milwaukee, WI, one of the nation's oldest and leading private college preparatory schools. One of his poems was chosen to be posted inside a Tulsa Transit city bus. He is a 2017 Woody Guthrie Poet with numerous publications of poetry and nonfiction. An adjunct professor at Rogers State University, he lives in Pryor, Oklahoma, where a Little League baseball field has been named in his honor.

Made in the USA
Lexington, KY
16 July 2018